Tпᴄ

CLASSROOM

Lessons on Life and Leadership from a
Texas High School Football Dynasty

Study Guide

Can You Master the Seven Traits of a Winner?

Clint Rutledge

What others are saying about *The Classroom...*

I've known my friend Clint Rutledge since our college days over 20 years ago. Clint's book, the Classroom, isn't just about his legendary father's coaching ability - it's about the virtues and the character that truly make a person great.

Chip Gaines of HGTV's *Fixer Upper*

Growing up with deep roots in coaching at every level, I can really relate to Clint Rutledge's message in this book, and he didn't have to look far to find his inspiration. There is not a better man in the coaching profession than Clint's dad, D. W., who is a perfect example of what a coach can mean in a young person's life. Throughout my career, we always tried to run our program on the core values of communication, trust and respect. This book is about faith, responsibility and accountability. It is a blueprint of 'how to' when it comes to making a lasting difference.

Mack Brown
Author of *One Heartbeat: A Philosophy of Teamwork, Life and Leadership*
College Football Analyst for ESPN
Head Coach at the University of Texas 1998-2013

"As a product of the actual Classroom under Coach D.W. Rutledge, I can tell you first hand that this book will have a positive impact on your life. I love Clint Rutledge like a little brother. I remember him at practice when I played for his dad. I remember watching him win two State Championships as a player. And now, he has written a great book that will challenge you to your core. You'll be better as a result of reading it. The Classroom is a special book.

Derwin L. Gray
Author of *Hero: Unleashing God's Power in a Man's Heart (2010), Limitless Life: You Are More Than Your Past When God Holds Your Future (2013), Crazy Grace for Crazy Times Bible Study (2015),* and *The High-Definition Leader (2015).*
Pastor of Transformation Church
Former NFL Player
Former Judson Rocket

Sports are the best life "classroom" and coaches play the role of teaching those invaluable lessons of life. Clint has captured the essence of this as told through the eyes of a man who played for his father — legendary Texas High School Football Coach DW Rutledge. I highly recommend this book to any Coach, father, or young man who wants to learn those things that are most important in life.

Chad Hennings

3 time Super Bowl Champion

Air Force A-10 Pilot

Author of "Forces of Character"

Clint's Rutledge's book, "The Classroom" doesn't fit into a category, it creates one! Rare is the author who effectively communicates both substance and sizzle. He's done some heavy lifting on the leadership front without compromising the need to entertain the reader. He masterfully introduces us to the so called "soft" leadership skills that produce smarter more resilient people. Touchdown!

Spencer Tillman

Author of "Scoring in the Red Zone"

All-American Running Back at Oklahoma

Former NFL Running Back

College Football Analyst for Fox Sports

Wow! Classroom indeed! I really enjoyed reading this book by Clint Rutledge. It is a wonderful addition to coaching literature and the process of human development and leadership.

Joe Ehrmann

Author of "Inside Out Coaching"

Subject of New York Times Bestseller *Season of Life* by Jeffrey Marx

Named one of The 100 Most Influential Sports Educators in America by the Institute for International Sport

"Some of life's most valuable lessons can be learned through the world of sports. The greatest coaches are those who recognize the value of teaching those lessons to their kids on a daily basis. Even more importantly, we as fathers need to be teaching these things to our kids. In "The Classroom" Clint Rutledge captures the lessons his father taught him and thousands of other young men for nearly 20 years. They are valuable truths that will help you be successful at anything you do. I recommend this book to any coach, parent, or kid that is looking to get better at living the game of life."

Brad McCoy
Author of *Home Field Advantage: A Playbook on Life, Leadership and Legacy*
Athletic Director for the Flippen Group
Father of Chance, Case, and Colt McCoy

Table of Contents

Welcome 11

Session 1 – Where are You Now? 15

Session 2 – The Power of Attitude 25

Session 3 – Self-Evaluation.................................... 35

Session 4 – Expectations 41

Session 5 – Goal Setting 47

Mastering The Seven Traits of a Winner 53

Session 6 – Courage... 59

Session 7 – Character 73

Session 8 – Persistence 87

Session 9 – Commitment 101

Session 10 – Difference Maker 115

Session 11 – Leadership 127

Session 12 – Focus 141

A Call to Coaches 157

About the Author 163

Notes 165

Welcome

Welcome to The Classroom Study Guide! You are about to start a journey that has changed the lives of thousands of Coaches and young people over the last 30 years. What started out as a program in an old room above a gym in Converse, Texas has now been shared all over the world. While there are some insights to be gained from this program, you will quickly find that there is nothing revolutionary in these pages. Instead, it is a step by step process, that when put together, can change the course of your life.

This study guide was written to accompany the book. Although the study guide can stand on its own in many ways, each of the principles that you will be going through are explained in much more detail in the book. Each one of the sessions include some comments from the Coach in the story, but the comments included are not in their entirety. You will benefit the most if you read the book as you work through the study guide.

How to Use this Study Guide

Each session includes three sections.

Insight on the Topic

The first section is intended to give a brief description of the topic to remind you of the Coach's comments in the book.

Personal Reflection

The second session is a time for you to think through how the topic applies specifically to you. There are questions to prompt your thoughts and spaces to write your answers. This guide is intended to become a journal of lessons you are learning so write, highlight, make notes, and make it yours.

Group Discussion

This is a time for you to discuss the topic as a group. If you are doing this as a Coaching Staff, then use these questions as a time to discuss the state of your team during a staff meeting. If you are doing this as a team, then split up with your position coach and take some time to go through this as a unit. Smaller groups give more people a chance to talk and provide their insight. At the end of the group discussion, come together as a team and discuss your primary take away from the session.

Thank you for taking the time to invest in yourself and your team. My prayer is that your life will be blessed in multiple ways as you go through this study. As my dad always says, "there are two types of education in this world, the first teaches you how to make a living and the second teaches you how to live." That is the greatest value that athletics can bring to any life, school, or career. Sports teach us how to live, how to persevere, how to compete with class, and how to encourage others. May this study guide be a link that brings sports and life together in a way that compels you to be better at both.

Clint Rutledge

Session 1

Where are you now?

How Is Your Heart?

In Chapter 2 of *The Classroom*, the Coach tells a story found in Chapter 8 of the Gospel of Luke. It is one of Jesus' parables where he teaches on the condition of a person's heart.

"A farmer went out to sow some seed and as he threw the seed out, some of it landed on the road and birds came and ate it up. Some of the seed landed amongst the rocks and as the seed began to grow, the roots had nothing which to hold on too, and it soon withered and died. Still some of the seed landed on fertile soil but also amongst the thorns. As this seed began to grow, the thorns soon choked it out, and it died as well. Finally, some of the seed landed on fertile soil that was free from obstruction, and that seed grew and grew to produce a crop 40, 50, even 100 times more than was sown. He who has ears to hear, let him hear…

I ask you young men today as you sit in this Classroom, do you have ears to hear? If you do, which one of these examples will you be? How is your heart today?

Jesus later told his disciples the meaning of the parable. He said the seed is the word of God and the different types of soil are like the different types of hearts that you find in people. I believe the seed can also represent a good message that someone who genuinely cares about you, is trying to plant into your life. The question is what type of heart will you choose to have?

Are you hard hearted like the road? Are you the type of person who is awarded an opportunity to hear something that is good and can change your life, but you simply ignore it? Maybe you ignore it because you already have it all figured out. Maybe you ignore it because you have already filled your heart with too much hatred, distrust, or anger to put anything else in there. Maybe you just ignore it because you are too lazy to change. Whatever the reason, I pray that as we enter The Classroom phase of our offseason, and good strong messages are presented to you, that you will not be hard hearted.

Or, Is your heart like the soil amongst the rocks? These are the people that hear the message and they recognize it as something good, but they are shallow. They don't have enough substance and depth to let it take root in their life. Eventually, when times get tough and adversity hits, the message withers and dies because there was nothing of substance for it to hold on to. I challenge you today to move past immaturity, create some depth in your life, and listen to the positive things being presented.

Or, is your heart like the good soil amongst the thorns. These are the people that hear the message and they recognize it as good and something that can benefit their life. They even have some depth about them so that the seed has room to grow and take hold. However, they have made poor choices in their friends. As the seed takes hold in their life, their friends soon choke out the good message and replace it with the wrong things. Their friends lead them away from the good things God wants for their life and takes them down a road filled with drugs, alcohol, pornography, and all other kinds of destructive behaviors. Young men, I want you to understand that how you choose your friends is critically important. It is an unwritten law that will forever be true, you will become like the people you hang around.

The final example is that of the fertile soil. My hope is that is where you find yourself today. I want you to have a heart that is hungry to listen, and learn, and get better. I pray that you have depth in your life and you have surrounded yourself with the right kind of people who are going to encourage you to get better and support you along the way. If you come here today, and tomorrow, and the next day with that kind of heart, I can promise you, you will get better. You will leave this program a better person and you will end up producing a hundred times more in your life than was ever sown here in The Classroom.

Personal Reflection

What is the condition of your heart today? Imagine for a moment that you were asked to send a survey to the 10 people closest to you in your life. In the survey, they were required to anonymously and honestly answer these 5 questions about you:

Over the course of this past month, would you say he/she has been...

1) Predominately joyful or predominately grouchy?

2) More selfish or more giving?

3) Honest and forthright or deceitful and manipulative.

4) Kind and forgiving or harsh and vengeful?

5) Fun to be around or miserable to be around.

Remember, "what you do speaks so loud, we can't hear what you say." It is your actions and reactions to normal life situations that truly reveal the condition of your heart. So, how would you rate your heart today?

1) Hard Hearted
2) Shallow
3) Fertile but Surrounded by Thorns
4) Fertile

If you are not where you want to be, that is ok. It is not too late to make a change. If you are on the right track, that is great! Keep it up. Either way, let's take a moment to define and clarify what kind of person you want to be.

_____ (your name) is a person who is…

_____

_____

_____

_____

_____

_____

Discussion Questions

Why do you think some people choose to be Hard Hearted?

_____

_____

_____

_____

Would you describe most of the kids in your school as hard hearted, shallow, good hearted but easily influenced in the wrong direction, or good hearted?

_____

_____

_____

_____

They say most great teams have "one heart beat." If that is the case, what is the condition of the heart of your team as a whole?

_____

_____

_____

_____

For someone to be an effective leader, what kind of heart do you think they need to have? Why?

_____

_____

_____

_____

What do you think is the key to making sure you personally continue to have a fertile heart?

_____

_____

_____

_____

Notes

Session 2

The Power of Attitude

In Chapter 3 of the <u>The Classroom</u>, Coach addresses the topic of Attitude.

What is Attitude?

So, if attitude is that important, what exactly is it? Webster's dictionary defines attitude as "habits of the mind which one displays." My favorite definitions though come from players just like you guys. Some players have said, "I think attitude is the choices that you make." Others have said, "I think attitude is how you think, or how you approach something." Personally, I think attitude is how we choose to look at life and that is a result of how we think.

A positive attitude is thinking the right thoughts, making the right choices and developing the right habits. A negative attitude is the exact opposite. It is thinking negative thoughts, making negative choices, and developing negative habits.

Your attitude is the little yes's and no's that you choose each day which determine who you truly are and what you will eventually become.

Let's put this in practical terms though. Let me give you some examples of attitudes that we choose each day. We can choose to be enthusiastic or have a sour disposition. We can choose an attitude of hard work or a lazy attitude. We can choose to love or hate to be committed or simply go along with the crowd. We can choose persistence or we can choose to quit. Finally, we choose an attitude of discipline or we can choose to take the easy way out.

The Process of Who We Become
The difference between accomplishment and failure is having the right attitude. Let me see if I can explain how it works. There is a process that we all go through day after day, month after month, year after year. The process goes like this: the things you put into your mind on a daily basis (the things you read, the shows you watch, the conversations you have) determines how you think - how you think determines the choices that you make - the choices that you make determines the habits that you develop - and the habits that you develop determines the person that you become.

If the process of who we become was a car, something that gets us from where we are to where we want to be, your attitude would be the gasoline. Your attitude is the fuel that runs the car. Just like high quality gas will help a car run longer and stronger and low-quality gas will run a car into the ground. A positive or negative attitude will determine where and how far the process will take you in life. A positive attitude will help you get to the places you want to go, and it will make the entire ride an enjoyable one. A negative attitude will cause you to break down and it will make the ride miserable for everyone around you.

One of my favorite quotes on attitude comes from Chuck Swindoll who says it much better than I ever could: "The longer I live the more I realize the impact of attitude on life. Attitude to me is more important than facts. It is more important than the past, than education, than money, than circumstances, than failures, than successes, than what other people think or say or do. It is more important than appearance, giftedness, or skill. It will make or break a company… a church… a home… a team. The remarkable thing is we have a choice every day regarding the attitude we embrace for that day. We cannot change our past… we cannot change the fact that people will act in a certain way.

We cannot change the inevitable. The only thing we can do is play on the one string we have, and that is our attitude… I am convinced that life is 10% what happens to me and 90% how I react to it. And so it is with you… we are in charge of our attitudes."

Personal Reflection

What does is the Webster's Dictionary definition of Attitude?

_____

_____

_____

What is YOUR definition of Attitude?

_____

_____

_____

How would you rate your overall Attitude in recent weeks? (1 being Terrible and 10 being Great)

    1 2   3   4   5   6   7   8   9   10

Fill in the blanks for the process that determines who we become:

The things you put into your _____ on a daily basis (the things you read, the shows you watch, the conversations you have) determines how you _____ - how you think determines the _____ that you make - the choices that you make determines the _____ that you develop - and the habits that you develop determines the _____ that you become.

Discussion Questions

Do you personally think that attitude makes that big of a difference?

_____

_____

_____

_____

Can you think of an example in your life where you approached something with a good attitude and succeeded or a bad attitude and struggled?

_____

_____

_____

_____

What is your typical attitude when it comes to practice?

_____

_____

_____

_____

What is your team's typical attitude when it comes to practice?

_____

_____

_____

_____

If your team was to approach practice with a Positive Attitude, how much better do you think you could be? Why?

_____

_____

_____

_____

PRACTICE ATTITUDE

Practice does not make perfect – practice makes permanent. No matter what you do, if you practice long enough it will become a part of you. Practice a bad habit and you will become great at a bad habit. Practice being second class and you will be second class. Practice being first class and you will be first class. The choices you make in tough situations will be the habits you develop. When you choose a habit you also choose the end result of that habit.

The habits we choose on a daily basis will ultimately determine what we become as a person. The habits we choose to practice will be the habits we will revert to when life gets tough. We all perform exactly as we practice.

Our practice attitude is the key to our success in anything we do. Remember, "What you do speaks so loud, I can't hear what you say." Albert Einstein once said, "Example is not the best way to teach, it is the only way." Leaders are leaders because of what they do, not what they say they are going to do. Every person must strive to be an example, demonstrating class, discipline, focus, and total effort.

When you practice, work to accomplish something – work to get better. Many people confuse activity with accomplishment. Putting in time or attending meetings ensures nothing. It matters not where you start – what matters is where you finish. Every practice, every day, is an opportunity for you to get better individually.

"But Effort? Nobody can judge that

Because Effort is Between

YOU and YOU."

Ray Lewis

Notes

Session 3

Self-Evaluation

In Chapter 4, Coach takes his team through a self-evaluation so they can establish where they are as individuals. Go through each attitude trait in The Classroom one at a time and read their description. After you read a description, rate yourself on that attitude trait. Your position coach will rate you on each attitude trait as well. Schedule a time to meet with your position coach and then two of you can compare your Evaluations.

Beginning of Chapter 4 of The Classroom:

"Ok, guys. We have firmly established two things so far.

> *1) You have to make a decision on the condition of your heart. There is only one choice if you truly want to be successful. You must have a fertile heart that is*

open to getting better. Doing so, means you are not hard hearted, you are not shallow, and you are choosing to surround yourself with the right friends.

2) Your attitude is the single most important factor in your success in anything you do in life. Your talent is of little significance if your attitude is not right. To have a positive attitude, you need to stop, consider your blessings and think of how different your life would be if those blessings didn't exist. It is through a heart of gratitude that we develop a great attitude.

Today, we will examine the Seven Traits of a Winner. Listen to the descriptions carefully because you will be asked to rate yourself on each of these attitude traits. Please be honest. Our goal today is to establish where we are. We will talk later about where we want to be. Let's start with Courage.

Self Evaluation Form

Name _____

Position _____ Date _____

"All our dreams can come true if we will just have the courage and dedication to pursue them." - Walt Disney

Rate yourself in the Seven Attitude traits listed below by circling the appropriate level

Courage:	Low	Below Average	Average	Above Average	High
Character:	Low	Below Average	Average	Above Average	High
Persistence:	Low	Below Average	Average	Above Average	High
Commitment:	Low	Below Average	Average	Above Average	High
Difference Maker:	Low	Below Average	Average	Above Average	High
Leadership:	Low	Below Average	Average	Above Average	High
Focus:	Low	Below Average	Average	Above Average	High

"A Hero is no braver than an ordinary man, but he is brave five minutes longer"

Ralph Waldo Emerson

Personal Reflection

Which Character Trait did you rate yourself the highest?
Why?

_____

_____

_____

Which Character Trait did you rate yourself the lowest?
Why?

_____

_____

_____

Which of these character traits would you to work on
developing in your own life first?

_____

_____

_____

What can you do to develop these character traits in your
own life?

_____

_____

_____

Discussion Questions

Which one of the character traits do you think is most important for a successful life? Why?

_____

_____

_____

Which one of the character traits do you think is most important for a successful team? Why?

_____

_____

_____

Do you think it is important to develop these character traits in your life? Why or why not?

_____

_____

_____

Which one of the character traits are you willing to commit to working on first?

_____

_____

_____

Notes

Session 4
Expectations

In Chapter 5, Coach goes over what he expects of his players and what the players can expect from their coaches.

"In 1929, Georgia Tech was playing against the University of California in the Rose Bowl. Georgia Tech had a defensive end by the name of Roy Reigals. Roy rushed in from the defensive right side, charging headlong for the quarterback when he got blindsided. The hit was so hard that he became disoriented. About that time, someone deflected a pass, which flew up in the air and came down in Roy's arms. The surprised Reigals took off at top speed, running for the goal line. He was thrilled! It was the first time he'd touched the ball all year, and now he was going to score. But on the three yard line, after running 63 yards he was tackled by one of his own teammates. It was only then that he discovered he'd been running in the wrong direction. For the rest of his life he was known as "Wrong Way Riegals."

At halftime, totally dejected, he sat in one corner of the dressing room unwilling to even talk to his teammates. No one thought he'd even come back out to play the second half. They thought he'd just give up. To everyone's surprise, not only did he come back out the second half, he had the greatest half of his career. When the game was over, Roy was asked, "How did you do it? We didn't even think you would have the courage to play the second half. Yet, you played the greatest half of your career?" Roy replied, "Oh, that's simple. My Coach came over to me as I was sitting in a corner by myself with my head down between my legs. I wanted to quit. But he grabbed me by the shoulders and pulled me up, looked me in the eye, and said something I couldn't shake. He said, "Roy, I believe in you. I expect a great game from you!" I realized that if my Coach believed in me, I couldn't let him down. So, I went back out and played with everything in me!"

Just like Roy's Coach believed in him and had expectations of him, even in the midst of his mistake, we believe in you guys and have certain expectations for each and every one of you. We don't expect you to be perfect any more than Roy's coach expected him to be perfect. We know mistakes will happen, but that doesn't mean we lower our expectations either. My hope is that you have certain expectations of yourself as well.

Personal Reflection

Who has highest expectations of you? Why?

_____

_____

_____

What do you expect of yourself?

_____

_____

_____

What does your family expect of you?

_____

_____

_____

What do the coaches expect of you?

_____

_____

_____

What does your Team expect of you?

_____

_____

_____

Discussion Questions

Do you see expectations as a burden or a benefit? Why?

_____

_____

_____

List 5 things good coaches should expect from their players

1. _____
2. _____
3. _____
4. _____
5. _____

List 5 things that Teammates should expect from each other

1. _____
2. _____
3. _____
4. _____
5. _____

Notes

Session 5
Goal Setting

In Chapter Six of The Classroom, Coach goes through the seven step process of Goal Setting.

Step 1 – State the Goal
You need to clearly define what it is you are working towards and you need to write it down.

Step 2 – Set a Deadline
The deadline is crucial because it doesn't leave the goal lingering out there forever as something you will do someday.

Step 3 – Identify the Obstacles
It is usually pretty easy to identify the things that will try and keep you from accomplishing your goal. The tough part is to not let this part of the exercise discourage you to the point where you think it cannot be done.

Step 4 – Identify the people or groups who can help you accomplish your goal
You want to know who your allies are. There are people out there who care about you and want to see you succeed. This

part of the goal setting process helps you to identify those people so you make sure you are staying on the right path and surrounding yourself with the right people.

Step 5 – List the Benefits of Achieving this Goal

You want to paint a picture in your mind of what life will be like once you accomplish your goal.

Step 6 – List the skills you will need to accomplish this goal

It is important to identify the skills you will need because you are defining what you need to work on.

Step 7 – Develop a Plan

At this point in the process you now know what you are working towards, what it is going to take to get there, what stands in your way, and who your allies are in the process. Now it is time to develop your plan for getting there. How are you going to overcome your obstacles and what do you need to accomplish each day to execute your plan? Here is how it translates for our Team Goal…

Goal Setting Worksheet

Name: _____

Type of Goal: Personal ____   Academic ____   Life _____

State Your Goal:

_____

Set a Deadline:

_____

Identify the Obstacles:

_____

_____

Identify the people who can help you accomplish this goal:

_____

_____

List the Benefits of Achieving this Goal:

_____

_____

List the Skills you will need to Achieve this Goal:

_____

_____

Identify your plan for achieving this Goal:

_____

_____

Personal Reflection

Did you learn anything new about goal setting through this exercise? If so, what was it?

_____

_____

_____

Why does it make a difference if you take the time to write your goal down?

_____

_____

_____

What are 3 other goals you have for your life?

1. _____

_____

2. _____

_____

3. _____

_____

How do your daily decisions now effect the likelihood of you accomplishing these goals?

_____

_____

_____

Discussion Questions

Do you prefer to set goals and go after them or just live life as it comes? Why?

_____

_____

_____

Do you see a benefit to taking the time to write down your goals and a plan for accomplishing them? Why or why not?

_____

_____

_____

Why do you think most people never take the time to write down their goals?

_____

_____

_____

What role does accountability have in accomplishing a goal? Who holds you accountable?

_____

_____

_____

Notes

Mastering The Seven Traits of a Winner

The last seven sections of this study guide will focus on mastering The Seven Traits of a winner. Before we move into Session 6 and the first trait of a winner, let's look at what Coach tells his team it is going to take for them to truly Master the Seven Traits…

Mastering each one of these traits is an ongoing process. You cannot follow a secret formula and wake up some day with a certificate showing that you have officially mastered courage, character, persistence, or any of the other traits. However, just like anything else in life, the more we choose courage, character, persistence, etc., the more it becomes a habit and a part of who we are - thus we master it over the course of our life.

There are three steps to mastering each one of the traits and the steps coincide with the process we have already discussed. Remember the process? What you put into your mind, determines how you think, how you think determines the choices that you make, the choices that you make determine the habits that you develop, and the habits that you develop determine the person that you become. The three steps that coincide with this process are: decide, define, and deliver. Here is how it works:

Decide

First you must decide that the trait is important and something you truly want to master. Once you make that decision, read the decision every day for 30 days when you wake up and before you go to bed. This will inundate your mind with strong thoughts regarding that specific character trait. At the same time, you must decide to guard what goes into your mind. Anything that could hinder the development of the trait in your life must be denied. Anything that could cultivate the trait should be consumed. For example, if you want to master courage, guard your mind against things that cause fear and apprehension, and fill your mind with things that empower you, lift you up, and produces confidence. Once you deny the bad and fill your mind with the good, your thoughts will begin to reflect what is going into your mind. If you have filled your mind with words and images that empower and encourage you, the next time you need to show courage in a situation, you will make the right choice because you have been thinking the right thoughts.

Define

Once you have made the decision that the trait is important, something you want to master, and you are going to act on that by guarding what goes into your mind; the next step is to define how you are going to act on that decision. Define or list the things that will weaken the trait in your life and then define or list the things that will develop the trait. In doing this, you will have identified the things you need to stay away from and the things you need to gravitate towards. There is no question that we live in an age where information is more readily available than it has ever been in history. There are lots of advantages to this but there are also disadvantages. Just because information is available doesn't mean it is worth our time, or that it is beneficial to consume it. It is just like food. There is an ice cream store not too far from here. Right next door to it is a donut shop. Both of those places are available to me anytime that I choose to eat a donut or buy some ice cream. In fact, I could have as many donuts and as much ice cream as I want any day that I want it. Just because they are there and available doesn't mean they are good for me. If I did not place some restrictions on myself on how often I ate donuts and ice cream, I would quickly become lethargic, overweight, unhealthy, and unproductive. Now more than ever, you must learn how to have discernment in your life. You have to decide what information you will choose to consume and what information you will choose to avoid. Defining or listing the things that will take you closer too or further away from having the traits of a winner will help you in discerning what goes into your mind and what does not.

Deliver

Finally, once you have made the decision that it is important, defined what you will allow into your mind and what you will avoid, you must deliver on what you say you are going to do. Typically, this is the toughest part. It is the same reason why people have such a hard time sticking with their New Year's Resolutions. However, if you are going to master the traits of a winner, you have to stick to your plan. Eventually, if you stick with it long enough, it will become a part of you. Your thoughts will be strong, which will lead to strong choices, which will lead to strong habits, which will lead to a stronger you – a winner in every aspect of your life.

So, let's put Decide, Define, and Deliver into action for our first Trait of a Winner – courage."

Notes

Session 6
Courage

A fair question for anyone to ask at this point is, "Do I really need this trait in my life?" Some would argue that courage is only necessary for military personnel or super heroes. Since you don't plan on fighting in a war in the next couple of months or participating in the next Avengers movie, do you really need to spend time on this trait?

It is a fair question.

Lets' look at the scenario that Coach presents to his players explaining why courage is especially important for young people.

Courage is the first trait of a winner. It takes courage to do what is right rather than what is popular. It takes courage to give everything you have to a cause knowing that you may succeed, or you may fail. It takes courage to stand up for what you believe, be a friend to a kid who is a little different from you, say no to drugs and alcohol when others seem to be running towards it. It takes courage to abstain from sex until marriage when it seems like everyone else's measure of a man is having as much sex as possible. It takes courage to live a life that is based on God's principles rather than what the world says you should be doing. It takes courage to be a winner!

To fully appreciate this trait though, it sometimes helps to look at the opposite side of the coin. What happens to the kid who doesn't show courage in those situations? Let's take the example of a party. You go to a party expecting to hang out with friends and have fun. When you arrive though, things are much different than you thought. It becomes evident very quickly that drugs and alcohol are present at the party. In fact, it seems like everyone there is drinking and trying the drugs. There is even a girl there that you have been hoping to impress. She and one of her friends walk up and hand you a beer and then asks if you if have ever smoked marijuana or tried some other kind of drug. You are caught off guard and not sure how to respond.

Do you do what you know is wrong thinking it will make a good impression, or do you risk being made fun of and say no thank you and walk away? Obviously, it takes courage to walk away, but what happens if you don't have courage in that moment? What if you conform and do what you know is wrong hoping to win the approval of that girl or some other person that you want to impress? The result is you start down a road that is very hard to ever come back from. You win her approval and you feel cool for the time being.

The next week you get invited to another party and you do the same thing. Again, you feel as though you are "fitting in" and accepted by this crowd. You are even developing a relationship with the girl you had your eye on. For several weeks, this pattern continues. At some point in the pattern though, you start to feel guilty for what you are doing because you know it is wrong. You decide to stop, and you say you can't make it to the next party. Your new "friends" pepper you with questions and do their best to talk you into coming. You do your best to make excuses and think you have talked yourself out of going.

However, the weekend shows up and you are trying to stick to your guns and not go. Something inside you starts to *crave the high you have been feeling from the drugs, the alcohol, and the approval of others who are doing the wrong thing. The craving persists until eventually you give in and go. In a matter of weeks, you have become addicted to something you swore you would never be a part of. It is an addiction that will follow you for the rest of your life. You aren't sure how it happened so fast, but you have become a person you do not want to be, and you do not see an easy way out.*

It can happen that quickly and it is a reality in the lives of way too many kids today. Most of those kids grow up to become adults with substance abuse problems. They even have families, but their families suffer because of their issues that all began when they were a teenager and they didn't have the courage to walk away. They didn't have the courage to go in the right direction despite what everyone else seemed to be doing.

While this could be considered an extreme scenario, it is happening every day in every community across the nation. It doesn't take much common sense to know that drugs and alcohol are not good for you. Yet, there are people every day who fall into their traps because they lack the courage to walk away.

Courage is where it all begins. To succeed in this life, you must have courage.

> It takes courage to walk away from the crowd.
> It takes courage to pursuit success at the risk of finding failure.
> It takes courage to learn a new skill, meet new friends, or start a new job.
> It takes courage to follow your dreams and pursuit your passions.
> It takes courage to get up in the morning and attack a new day after having a bad day.
> It takes courage to forgive.
> It takes courage to love.
> It takes courage to make a difference in this world.

Notes

Personal Reflection

In what areas of your life are you currently showing courage?

_____

_____

_____

In what areas of your life do you need to show more courage?

_____

_____

_____

What do you fear the most? Why?

_____

_____

_____

What can you do to face this fear?

_____

_____

_____

What does it mean to *en*courage someone? How can you encourage someone else today?

_____

_____

_____

FEAR is a **Reaction,**

Courage is a

Decision

Group Discussion

Why does it take courage to be a teenager today?

_____

_____

_____

_____

What are some things you can do to help your teammates or the kids you coach when it comes to showing courage?

_____

_____

_____

_____

Do you believe courage can be a habit? Why or why not?

_____

_____

_____

Why is courage important for a successful life?

_____

_____

_____

_____

Is it realistic to think you can be courageous in every situation? Then what is the point of trying to be courageous in any situation?

_____

_____

_____

_____

As Coach discussed with his players in the story, the key to mastering the seven traits is to decide, define, and deliver. Take a moment now to do this when it comes to Courage.

Courage

Decide

From this moment on, I choose to be courageous in the way I live my life. Just like the Lord told Joshua in the Bible when he was getting ready to take the Promised Land - "Be strong and **courageous**. Do not be afraid; do not be discouraged, for the LORD your God will be with you wherever you go." I recognize that there are uncertainties in life, just like there was for Joshua. Joshua knew he would face giants, walls, and adversities, but he could remain courageous because God was on his side. I know that God is on my side as well. He wants what is best for me. I have my own promised land to conquer. In conquering this land, I will face my own giants, I will run into my own walls, and I will face my own adversities. These things do not scare me. I will face them boldly. I will charge them just as David charged Goliath. I will not run from the obstacles that come before me. Instead, with God's guidance, I will form a plan and I will overcome each obstacle that blocks my path.

In the future, when I am faced with a choice of doing what is right or doing what is popular, I will always do what is right.

I am more concerned with what God thinks of me than what other people think. I will not be influenced by the direction in which others are running. Instead, I will listen to my conscience and I will follow God's guidance. I will do what it is right.

In showing courage, I realize that I might empower others around me to show courage as well. I take that responsibility seriously and I welcome the challenge. Most of the time, there are others in the room, on the field, or on the court that are waiting and hoping for someone else to have the courage to do the right thing. When someone else stands up and does what is right, they too feel encouraged and empowered to follow that other person's lead and go in the right direction. I will be that person. If my courage encourages another, it is all the more reason for me to do what is right.

I understand that courage is not the absence of fear. Like John Wayne said, "Courage is being scared, but saddling up anyway." Just because there are times in my life when I am afraid does not mean that I am not courageous. Fear is a part of life and it has its purpose. However, I refuse to let fear keep me from doing what needs to be done. Just as Paul says in 2

Timothy 1:7, "God did not create in me a spirit of timidity, but of power, of love, and of self-discipline." My self-discipline and my faith have the power to overcome my fear. I refuse to let fear of failure or the fear of others opinions stand in my way. I am Courageous, I am 1 out of 100, I trust in the Lord, and I know that He is with me always.

Define

I resolve to avoid the following things (certain TV Shows, Movies, Books, Music, things online, etc) that would seek to weaken my courage:

_____

_____

_____

_____

_____

_____

_____

_____

I resolve to seek out and pursue the following things (Books, Music, Movies, People, Shows, etc,) that will strengthen my courage:

_____

_____

_____

_____

_____

_____

_____

_____

Deliver

In signing my name, I commit to reading this decision every morning and every night for 30 days, guard my mind from things that will weaken my courage, and fill my mind with things that will strengthen my courage.

_____   _____

Signature   Date

Session 7

Character

Character has been defined many ways. Some people say Character is who you are when no one is watching. The dictionary defines Character as the mental and moral qualities distinctive to an individual. Another definition says that Character is the group of qualities that make a person, group, or thing different from others. Let's look at what Coach had to say to his team about Character...

One of my favorite authors, Andy Andrews, compares integrity, morality, and character in his book The Noticer Returns. In his book, the main character of the story, Jones, is teaching a lesson to some young parents about the most important traits we need to develop in our kids. In the midst of the discussion, he reveals to them the difference between the three traits. "Integrity," he says "is defined as trustworthy, dependable, and capable of doing the task for which it has been given, which is a fine thing to be. However, a fire escape can have Integrity. Morality," he continues, "is not doing what is wrong. Again, that is a fine trait and we need more moral people in this world. However, you can stay in your house all day and not do anything wrong. Character on the other hand, is actively doing what is right."

I absolutely love that definition of character. It is actively doing what is right. That is truly what we need more in the world today. We need more people who see a need and find a way to meet it. In order to actively do what is right though, you have to have courage, which is why it was the first trait of a winner. Character is the second trait of a winner. The person who masters character is one who is continually looking to make a positive difference in his world. He is actively doing what is right. It is amazing how a sincere desire to do what is right – true character - can overcome any fear that may be holding you back. The good news is this is a trait that can be developed, learned, or instilled in a person's life no matter how much they may have lacked character in the past. The best way I know to prove this is through a story that Paul Harvey once told. It is the story of a man named Big Bad Eddie O'Hare….

The speckles in the Pacific night sky were bombers. Nine twin-engine Japanese bombers, in formation, on course to their target: the aircraft carrier Lexington. Butch O'Hare could see them all clearly from the cockpit of his Grumman Wildcat F4F. He was their lone-wolf pursuer, tagging along in the darkness. If he did not seize the opportunity now to attack from the rear, his home base, the carrier Lexington, would be obliterated--sent to the ocean floor in fragments of twisted steel. So Butch gripped the controls, palms sweating in anticipation of what he knew he must do. The engine roared and the Wildcat lunged for its prey. Before it was over, five of the nine Japanese bombers had been dumped into the Pacific. Butch was ripping away at a sixth when he ran out of ammunition . . . and his comrades arrived to finish the job. That was February 29, 1942, and the daring of Lieutenant Commander Edward Henry "Butch" O'Hare . . . the Navy's number-one World War II ace, the first naval aviator to ever win the Congressional Medal of Honor. A year later, Butch went down in aerial combat. But his home towners would not allow the memory of that heroic accomplishment to die. So the next time you fly into Chicago's O'Hare International Airport, you'll know for whom it was named, and why. What you don't yet know is that you'll be passing through a shrine . . . a monument to a very special kind of love . . . and that's THE REST OF THE STORY.

Chicago. The Roaring Twenties. The time and territory of gangster Al Capone. And of all the Capone cronies . . . of all the unsavory soldiers who served in that army of crime . . . only one earned the nickname "Artful Eddie." Eddie was the fast lawyer's fast lawyer. Through his loopholes walked the most glamorous rogues in the gallery of gangland. In 1923, Eddie himself was indicted on an illegal booze deal, two hundred thousand dollars' worth, but he won his own reversal. Later, Al Capone picked up Eddie and put him in charge of the dog tracks nationwide. You see, Eddie had already swiped the patent on the mechanical rabbit. Pretty soon Artful Eddie, as the Capone syndicate representative, became known as the undisputed czar of illegal dog racing. Nothing could have been easier to rig in favor of the mob. Eight dogs running . . . overfeed seven . . . it was as simple as that. In no time, Artful Eddie became a wealthy man. Then, one day, for no apparent reason, Eddie squealed on Capone. He wanted to go straight, he told the authorities. What did they want to know? The authorities were understandably skeptical. Why should Artful Eddie, the pride of the underworld, seek to undermine his own carefully constructed dog-track empire? Didn't Eddie know what it meant . . . to rat on the mob? He knew. Then, what was the deal? What could he possibly hope to gain from aiding the *government that he didn't already have? Eddie had money. Eddie had power. Eddie had the pledged security of the one and only Al Capone. What was the hitch? That's when Artful Eddie revealed the hitch. There was only one thing that really mattered to him. He'd spent his life among the disreputable and despicable. After all was said and done, there was only one who deserved a break. His son. His son deserved better. Eddie decided it was finally time to do the right thing. So Eddie squealed . . . and the mob remembered . . . and in time, two shotgun blasts would silence him forever. Eddie never lived to see his dream come true. But it did. For as he cleansed the family name of the underworld stain, his son became acceptable too, and was eventually accepted by the Naval Academy. He became the flying ace who downed five bombers and went on to win the Congressional Medal of Honor. So the next time you fly into Chicago's O'Hare International Airport, remember Butch O'Hare . . . and his daddy, Edward J. "Artful Eddie," the crook who one day decided it was time to do the right thing . . . He paid with his own life for his son's chance to have something that cannot be bought. A name that is reputable.*

Although Butch O'Hare saved the lives of the men on that aircraft carrier, it was his father's decision to do the right thing that made his son's actions possible. So, you could say it was the character of Artful Eddie that eventually saved the lives of thousands of American young men. Eddie didn't always prove to have character, but he did prove in the end that character is something that can be developed if you only want it bad enough.

Personal Reflection

How do you define Character?

_____

_____

_____

What do you want your name to stand for?

_____

_____

_____

Why do you think Character is important for a good life?

_____

_____

_____

What can you do to develop your Character?

_____

_____

_____

What type of Character do you want your friends to have?

_____

_____

_____

Group Discussion

Discuss different definitions of Character and agree on one for your group.

_____

_____

_____

_____

Do you think Character makes a difference in the athletic world?

_____

_____

_____

_____

Do you think it is important for your team to have Character? Why?

_____

_____

_____

_____

If you were to mentor someone 5 years younger, what would you tell them about the importance of Character?

_____

_____

_____

_____

What can you do as a group to challenge each other to continue improving your individual Character?

_____

_____

_____

_____

Character, not

Circumstance

MAKES THE **Person**

As Coach discussed with his players in the story, the key to mastering the seven traits is to decide, define, and deliver. Take a moment now to do this when it comes to Character.

Character

Decide

Beginning today, I choose to live a life of character. I choose to actively do what is right. When I see a need, I will do everything in my power to meet that need. It can be something as simple as picking up a piece of trash, or it can be as bold as defending someone who is being unjustly treated. I refuse to be an inactive bystander to life. The world is in need of people who are willing to do the right thing. I am one of those people.

I am a person of character. I value the name I have been given. My name will be whatever I choose to make it. I choose to make it great. As it says in Proverbs Chapter 22 verse 1, "A good name is more desirable than great riches..." My name, my life will be defined by my character, and my character will be defined by my actions. What I do speaks so loud no one can hear what I say. My actions are also a representation of what is truly in my heart. I will therefore choose my actions carefully and guard against foolish decisions just as I have committed to guard what goes into my mind.

My actions will not be motivated by winning the approval of others. Rather, they will be motivated by living up to the standards I have set for myself. I have set my standards high for a reason and I refuse to lower them. Even on the days when my standards seem unattainable, I will continue to strive towards them. I fully understand that living a life defined by character is not easy, but I am up to the challenge. I understand that strong character results in a strong name and bad character results in a bad name. I will have a strong name. I will guard my actions with care. I will live a life defined by actively doing what is right. I will live a life of character.

Define

I resolve to avoid the following things that would weaken my character or ruin my name:

_____

_____

_____

_____

_____

I resolve to seek out and pursue the following things that will strengthen my character and give credibility to my name:

_____

_____

_____

_____

_____

_____

_____

Deliver

In signing my name, I commit to reading this decision every morning and every night for 30 days, guard my life from things that will weaken my character, and fill my life with things that will strengthen my character.

_____

Signature   Date

Session 8

Persistence

How well do you handle adversity? When things don't go your way, do you kick and scream, whine and complain, or do you suck it up and get back to work. We live in a world where the trait of persistence is becoming less and less prevalent.

Most people today are looking for instant gratification, and when they don't get what they want as quickly as they want, they give up and move on to something easier. For those rare individuals who are willing to put in the work and persist in the face of adversity, there are countless rewards in their future.

How do you measure up when it comes to persistence? It is not a trait that gets easier the more you display it. It is tough, but it is worth the effort. Let's look at what Coach had to say about the trait of Persistence…

Tenacious, driven, persistent. All words that represent the third trait of a winner. It is the refusal to quit no matter the odds. When adversity strikes, a winner will always fight back. If a winner gets knocked down, he gets back up and gets right back in the fight. One of my favorite stories of persistence has become a staple of our teams. For some teams, this story becomes their defining trait. For you guys, it remains to be seen. You cannot claim to be persistent. You can only prove to be persistent – just like the hero in our story….

There once was an evangelist who loved to hunt so he went out and bought two top notch bird dogs. The dogs were big, strong, and athletic dogs. The evangelist loved those dogs. Each morning he would wake up and look out of his kitchen window at his dogs while he was drinking his coffee. One morning, he was watching his dogs when he noticed something coming down the back alley way. As he looked closer, he noticed it was a short, stout, pudgy looking bulldog that was snorting and shuffling down the alley and toward his bird dogs.

The evangelist quickly became concerned that the little bulldog was going to squeeze under his fence and get into a fight with his two bird dogs. As he got up to go and scare the dog away, he ended up changing his mind. He thought to himself, "I will just let that little bulldog learn a lesson he won't soon forget. That way I won't have to worry about him coming back anymore."

Sure enough, the little bulldog stopped at the fence and looked at the two bird dogs. Some barking and trash talking took place between the two parties until the bulldog decided he would just squeeze under the fence and settle the matter. A fight quickly ensued and the two bird dogs were all over that little bulldog. There was dust and bulldog hair flying everywhere. When the little bulldog had had all he could take, he squeezed under the fence and ran home licking his wounds from that first day.

The next morning, as the evangelist was drinking his coffee, he couldn't believe what he saw. At exactly the same time, that little bulldog came snorting and shuffling down the alley way towards his two bird dogs. The bulldog stopped at the fence, the two parties barked and talked trash until the little bulldog decided to squeeze under the fence and settle the matter again. Just like the day before, the dogs went after each other. Again, there was dust and bulldog hair flying everywhere. When the little bulldog had had all he could take, he squeezed under the fence and ran home licking his wounds from the second day.

The third day, the same thing happened. At exactly the same time, the little bulldog came snorting and shuffling down the alley. He squeezed under the fence and dust and bulldog hair flew everywhere. When he had had all he could take, he ran home licking his wounds from the third day.

The following morning the evangelist had to leave before the sun came up to go on a trip that lasted two weeks. When he returned home and his wife picked him up from the airport, the two began talking about everything that had been happening at home.

In the course of the conversation, the evangelist asked his wife, "Whatever happened to that little bulldog that kept coming around?" His wife smiled and said, "You wouldn't believe it! Every single day that little bulldog came at the same time to fight your two bird dogs. He never missed a day and he never missed a fight.

It has gotten to the point now though that your two bird dogs are so tired of fighting that little bulldog that when they hear him come snorting and shuffling down the alley, they start whining and run straight for your basement. That little bulldog squeezes under the fence and struts around the back yard like he owns it! He drinks their water when he wants to drink their water, he eats their food when he wants to eat their food, and he even lies around in their favorite spots. He doesn't go home until he decides that he is ready to go home. It is then and only then that your two bird dogs will re-appear in the yard. I have never seen anything like it!"

The little bulldog had staying power. He was tenacious. He was persistent. It didn't matter that he got whipped the first time he got in the fight. It didn't matter that he got whipped the second time or the third time or the fourth time. He refused to quit. Every day, he got back up and got back in the fight. Where do you find yourself today? This world has a way of trying to beat us down. Have you been whipped at something recently? If you have, shake it off and get back in the fight.

Whatever challenges you are facing today, don't give up. Take it one day at a time and keep battling. You never know just how close you are to breaking through. Take some time now to do a little personal reflection and group discussion.

Personal Reflection

What is the biggest challenge you are currently facing?

_____

_____

_____

Do you struggle with staying persistent?

_____

_____

_____

What helps you stick with it when you would rather quit?

_____

_____

_____

What goals do you currently have where you know persistence will be necessary for success?

_____

_____

_____

Who do you know that can hold you accountable when it comes to staying persistent?

_____

_____

_____

Group Discussion

Why is it so hard to be persistent?

_____

_____

_____

_____

Who is the most persistent person you know? Why?

_____

_____

_____

_____

How do you know when you should persist or when it is time to simply try something different?

_____

_____

_____

_____

Why is it important for you team to be persistent?

_____

_____

_____

_____

How will persistence play a roll in the success of your team this year?

_____

_____

_____

_____

Winners never quit

AND QUITTERS **never Win**

As Coach discussed with his players in the story, the key to mastering the seven traits is to decide, define, and deliver. Take a moment now to do this when it comes to Persistence.

Persistence

Decide

I refuse to quit. I am persistent in all of my efforts. I fully recognize that life will try to knock me down and sometimes it will succeed. Adversity may come in the form of losses, failures, criticism, setbacks, or disappointments but it will not deter me from getting up the next day and getting back in the fight. Every morning that I get out of bed, I will remind myself that when it comes to dreams – "you never can tell how close you are, it may be near when it seems afar." I will work as though my dream could come true at any moment. It could be right around the corner or the result of my next opportunity. When that opportunity comes, I will be prepared because I have stayed in the fight.

Adversity will not defeat me. I will use it to become wiser and stronger. Criticism will not deflate me. The words of critics will inspire me to work harder and longer. I realize that no city ever built a statue of a critic because somewhere along the way the critic quit on his dreams and now tries to keep others from theirs. Their tactics will not work on me. I am destined to do something significant with my life. The only thing standing in my way is time. I will use that time to build depth in my life just like the bamboo tree. Each day, each hour, each minute that I work adds depth to my life and strength to my roots. Even when I can't see that something great is happening, I will continue to have faith that something good is on its way. It is through that faith that I will continue to dream, continue to work, and refuse to quit. I will stay in the fight, I will refuse to quit, I will strengthen my roots. I am persistent.

Define

I commit to avoiding the following things that would weaken my resolve or cause me to want to quit:

_____

_____

_____

_____

_____

_____

_____

I commit to seeking out and pursuing the following things that will strengthen my resolve and motivate me to remain persistent in my efforts:

_____

_____

_____

_____

_____

_____

_____

_____

Deliver

In signing my name, I commit to reading this decision every morning and every night for 30 days, guard my life from things that will weaken my resolve, and fill my life with things that will motivate to keep working and help me to refuse to quit.

_____

Signature   Date

Session 9
Commitment

Who is the better friend – one who is committed to you no matter what or one who is with you only when things are going well? Who is the better teammate – one who exhibits a good attitude and supports the team win or lose, or one who is all in when things are going well but complains and gives up when things don't go his way? Who is the better husband and father – one who remains faithful to his wife and kids and works to provide for his family through good times and bad times, or one who sticks around when life is easy but disappears as soon as life gets tough?

In each one of these scenarios, the answer is obvious. The committed friend is the better friend. The committed teammate is the better teammate and the committed Husband and Father is the better Husband and Father. If the answer is so obvious, why isn't everyone a good friend, a good teammate, or a good man? That answer is also obvious – Commitment isn't easy. Commitment is tough. It takes work, but it is worth it in the end. Let's look at what Coach had to say to his team about Commitment…

There was once a man who got lost in the desert. Sunburned, dehydrated, and literally dying of thirst, he happened over the top of a sand dune and found a weather beaten old shack. He stumbled over to the run down shack and collapsed against it, exhausted and defeated. As he leaned his head back against the hot tin of the shed he looked to his right and saw nothing but sand. As he turned his head to his left, he looked to the end of the shack and couldn't believe his eyes. He was certain his mind was playing tricks on him but he crawled to the other end of the shack anyway.

As he reached over, he was amazed to find out that his mind wasn't playing tricks on him at all. There in his grasp was a water canteen and it was full of water! He couldn't believe his good fortune. He shook it several times thoroughly enjoying the sound of the water he was about to drink. However, as he unscrewed the lid and began to place the canteen to his mouth something stopped him. He noticed that there was something written on the top of the canteen. It was as though someone had left him a message. He lowered the canteen and then carefully read the inscription. It said:

You have to prime the pump with the water in the jug!

"Prime the pump?" he said to himself. "What does that mean?" He began to look around for some kind of pump. He looked and looked until his eyes settled on something about 50 feet away from the shack. Sure enough, there it was. It was an old water pump that had to be cranked by hand. He remembered his grandfather showing him how one of those worked years ago.

All of a sudden, he realized he had a choice to make. He could drink the water that was currently in the jug, which was something he desperately wanted to do, or he could take a chance and pour the water down the pump to try and prime it. He thought and thought about his decision. If he drank the water in the canteen, he would live a day or two more and he would satisfy his thirst for the moment, but he probably wouldn't make it out of the desert.

However, if he took a chance, poured the water down the pump, primed it, and it worked, he could still satisfy his thirst, but he would also be able to refill all of his canteens and make it out of the desert. The risk though, was that it wouldn't work and he would have wasted the water that was right in front of him.

After much fretting and fighting with himself, he decided to take a chance. He went over to the pump, said a little prayer, and then began pouring the water down the pump. As he reached for the handle, he said another little prayer. His hand wrapped around the hot metal of the pump and recoiled from the heat. Determined to give it a try though, he grabbed the handle again ignoring the pain, and he began to crank it up and down up and down.

For 5 minutes he cranked the handle and nothing happened. Due to his weakened state, he was quickly becoming exhausted. Sweat rolled down his forehead and the sides of his cheeks. He stepped back breathing heavily staring at the pump and cursing it for taking his water. He stepped forward again and again he cranked the handle up and down up and down. Again, nothing happened. Once again he stepped back and stared at the pump, but this time his tears mixed with his sweat as he knew his life depended on what he was doing.

Finally, one last time he reached down and grabbed the pump. He began to crank up and down up and down. He cranked and he cranked and he cranked. At the moment he was about to collapse from exhaustion and despair, a drop of water appeared on the edge of the pump. With a new found sense of urgency, he continued to crank and a small trickle of water began to fall. Now it seemed as though the harder he cranked, the more water was flowing from the pump.

Finally, when water was gushing out of the old pump, he reached over, filled his hands and drank to his heart's content. The water was cold and he could feel it running down his hot and tired body and into his stomach. He had never tasted anything so good and had never felt so relieved.

When he could drink no more, he refilled all of his canteens. Lastly, he refilled the old canteen that he had found and he screwed the lid back on top. He said a prayer of thanks and he went to lay it back in its original spot for the next weary traveler. Before he set it down though, something came across his mind. He picked the canteen back up and pulled out his knife. Below the original inscription, he added this:

Believe me, it really works! But, you have to pour it ALL IN before you can get anything out!

So it is with each and every one of our lives. The greatest things in life come when we are willing to give everything we have to something. That is what commitment is. Commitment isn't saying you will do something when it is easy, but never following through when it gets tough. Commitment is pouring everything you have into something even when you aren't sure what the outcome is going to be. Commitment is refusing to quit when things aren't working out the way you thought they would or the way you think you deserve. Commitment is pushing through fatigue, hopelessness, and frustration to find bigger blessings than you could have ever imagined on the other side.

One of the secrets to staying Committed is identifying your motivation. When your motivations are based on selfish desires, your commitment will wane. When your motivations are based on those you love and respect, your commitment and your potential become limitless. Challenge yourself today to live a life of commitment and service rather than weakness and selfishness.

Personal Reflection

Who are the most important people in your life?

_____

_____

_____

_____

How do your good decisions effect those people? How do your bad decisions effect those people?

_____

_____

_____

_____

Do you believe Commitment can be a habit? Why?

_____

_____

_____

_____

What do you think is the secret to being a Committed person?

_____

_____

_____

_____

Think back to the process we discussed several sessions ago. How do the things you put into your mind on a daily basis ultimately have an effect on your commitment to those around you?

_____

_____

_____

_____

COMMITMENT IS A series

of Daily Choices

Group Discussion

How can you tell if a person is committed to the Team?

_____

_____

_____

_____

Can you consistently win if you do not have players on the team who are committed to the Team? Why?

_____

_____

_____

_____

How do you choose your friends? Is commitment a factor in who you choose to hang around?

_____

_____

_____

_____

What do you think is the secret to a Man or Woman staying committed to their family?

_____

_____

_____

_____

What are you willing to commit to your Team this season?

_____

_____

_____

_____

As Coach discussed with his players in the story, the key to mastering the seven traits is to decide, define, and deliver. Take a moment now to do this when it comes to Commitment.

Commitment

Decide

I am a committed and loyal person. If I say I am going to do something, the people around me can rest assured that it will get done. I fully realize that it is easy to commit to something when life is easy and the goal seems fun. However, remaining committed to something when life gets challenging, is a completely different story. It is in those moments where commitment is truly tested that I will rise to the top. I will prove my commitment in pushing forward and remaining faithful to what I said I would do.

When I commit to something or someone, they will get everything that I have. I will pour all that I am and all that I can be in to that task or relationship that I have committed to. I refuse to hold anything back. Some people will hold back on giving their best effort so they can look as though they weren't trying too hard or they didn't care that much – just in case they fail at what they are doing. I am not one of those people. I do not fear failure. If I fail while giving everything that I have, then I will step back, learn my lessons, and then try again.

Commitment is not proven through easy successes. Commitment is proven through failures, bumps in the road, and overcoming challenges. That is who I am and what I do. I learn from failures, I climb over bumps in the road, and I use challenges as stepping stones to greater success.

My commitment is strengthened through the people and things that I value most in my life. I understand that selfishness will seek to destroy those relationships that I hold dear and thus weaken my commitment. I will not allow selfishness to govern how I think. When selfishness strikes, I will fight back. I will choke it out by reminding myself of those who are counting on me and the joy that will come when I fulfill my commitments. I will not be defined by selfishness. I am loyal. I pour everything I have into what I say I will do. I am committed.

Define

I commit to avoiding the following things that would tempt me to waver on my commitments:

_____

_____

_____

_____

_____

_____

_____

I commit to seeking out and pursuing the following things that will strengthen my resolve and motivate me to remain true to my commitments:

_____

_____

_____

_____

_____

Deliver

In signing my name, I commit to reading this decision every morning and every night for 30 days, guarding my life from things that will weaken my resolve, and filling my life with things that will help me to fulfill my commitments.

_____

Signature   Date

Session 10

Difference Maker

There are many out there who would argue that our society has been in a steady state of moral decline for many years now. There are numerous reasons that people could justify that point of view. However, whatever side of the argument that you find yourself on, there is no disputing the fact that our society could always use more positive difference makers.

Many young people today are conditioned to keep their head down and do their own thing. The popular opinion is to not have an opinion. If something is wrong, we are taught to look the other way rather than find a way to make a difference. Making a Difference doesn't mean you have to go on a political crusade or start condemning people for their poor choices. In fact, it is quite the opposite. Let's look at what Coach has to say about being a difference maker...

Each one of you guys has been given an incredible opportunity to be a difference maker in the lives of others. My question to you is, what are you going to do with that opportunity? I sincerely hope you will not waste it. Our country is in dire need of young men who are determined to get out there and be a force for good in our society. Our communities need young men who are willing to step up and lead their families faithfully, be an active part of the community, and to truly be a difference maker in the lives of those around them.

I enjoy watching ESPN's 30 for 30 films. There is one on Bill McCartney who used to be the Head Coach at Colorado and then went on to start Promise Keepers. At one point in the film, McCartney shows us what he used to say to his recruits when he would bring them to Colorado. At the time, Colorado had been a terrible football team for many years. Nebraska and Oklahoma were the national powerhouses in college football. McCartney said, I would take the recruits to a spot that had magnificent views of the mountains, I would put my arm around them and say, "If you go to Oklahoma or Nebraska, you may just be another guy. You will be another number with a Jersey. BUT, if you come to Colorado YOU CAN BE A DIFFERENCE MAKER! Then we can go to Nebraska and we can go to Oklahoma and we can whip them in their own back yard, but we need you to do it!

What do you think God would say if he were recruiting you to be a difference maker in our world today? I think it would go something like this....

Jesus would bring you in and put His arm around you. He would say, "Things aren't great in America right now. There is a lot of selfishness, lack of morality, parents are giving up on their kids, kids are giving up on their parents, poor work ethic has become common place, and character has become less apparent. Right now, the devil thinks he is winning. I have got a surprise for him though. I am building a team and I want you to be on it. By all means, you could just go with the flow, ease through life without making any waves, you could just be another number with a jersey. I have to tell you though, that is not why I made you. That is not why I designed you the way I did. I created you to be a difference maker! I created you to be infuential in the lives of others! YOU can be a force for good in a world desperately in need! YOU could be a major player on my team! America is not lost, it is simply poised for a great comeback. The good guys are about to start winning again, but we need you on our team, we need you to join the fight! What do you think? Are you ready to commit and play for the good guys? It is time to get in the game, take a stand, do something good in the life of someone else, and then go find someone else to help. It really isn't that complicated. Just find those who need help and start helping."

The best way to make a difference is to look for a way to meet the needs of someone in your family, your school, or your community. That need can be met through actions or simple words of encouragement. Either way, it is when we serve as an encouragement or find ways to meet the needs of others that we truly make a difference. Positive change has never been created by the "critics" who do nothing but talk and complain. Positive change comes when people ignore the critics and cynics and start helping those around them. Become a difference maker in your community today!

Personal Reflection

Who is one person you know that could use some encouragement today?

_____

_____

_____

_____

What is a need in your family that you can meet?

_____

_____

_____

_____

What is a need in your school that you can meet?

_____

_____

_____

_____

What is a need in your community that you can meet?

_____

_____

_____

_____

Where do you want your life to make the biggest difference?

_____

_____

_____

_____

Do more things THAT MAKE YOU FORGET

to check your Phone

Group Discussion

Do you think it is possible for one person to make a difference?

_____

_____

_____

_____

Why is it that most young people fail to make a difference?

_____

_____

_____

_____

What are some needs in your school?

_____

_____

_____

_____

How can you help with those needs?

_____

_____

_____

_____

How different would your school look if the majority Coaches and kids were looking for way to help those around them? (How different would society look if that were the case?)

_____

_____

_____

_____

Be The Reason

Someone *Smiles*

TODAY!

As Coach discussed with his players in the story, the key to mastering the seven traits is to decide, define, and deliver. Take a moment now to do this when it comes to being a difference maker.

Difference Maker

Decide

I am a difference maker. While I may have big dreams and big goals, I refuse to sit around and wait for my "one big opportunity." Instead, I will get out there and make difference today, and I will do it one person and one conversation at a time. I understand that those who are out there making a difference on a smaller scale each and every day, are the ones who are actually making the biggest difference in world.

The times when I volunteer in the community, speak to a group of kids, or help someone else in need are the times when I am making the biggest difference. DL Moody once said, "There are many of us that are willing to do great things for the Lord, but few of us are willing to do little things." It is when I am content to do the small things for God that I actually become the most useful to Him because a heart that is willing to do the small things is more concerned with lives changed than credit given.

I know that God has a plan for my life and it is a great plan. I am not discouraged by what I see around me in society today. It is just the opposite. I am encouraged to go out and make a difference. Because I am on God's team, I will not be just another jersey with a number on it. Instead, I will be a Difference Maker. I will be a force for good in a world that needs it now more than ever. My life and my very existence at this point in history is not an accident. I am here to be a Difference Maker and that is what I intend to do.

I will leave the places I go better than how I found them. I will encourage others so that they are better for having come into contact with me. I will show kindness

and compassion to those in need. I will be a Difference
Maker!

Define

I commit to avoidng the following things that would inhibit my ability
to be a difference maker in the lives of others:

_____

_____

_____

_____

_____

_____

_____

I commit to seeking out and pursuing the following things that will
challenge and equip me to be a difference maker in the lives of others:

_____

_____

_____

_____

_____

_____

_____

Deliver

In signing my name, I commit to reading this decision every morning and every night for 30 days, guarding my life from things that will make me lazy, and filling my life with things that will help me be a difference maker in the lives of others.

_____

Signature   Date

Session 11

Leadership

Leadership. It is a topic discussed through countless books and speeches. People make their living by becoming "leadership experts." Business are always looking for innovative ways to approach the subject and Coaches are always looking for ways to develop new ones. It is a popular subject because it is an important subject. But, why is it so important? Is the cause of a great team truly based on the effect of great leaders? Let's see what Coach has to say about the subject of Leadership...

"The Key to any successful team, organization, church, school or family is effective leadership. Without effective leadership, it is nearly impossible to have a productive and successful organization. For some businesses, the structure clearly defines the leaders, everyone knows who is in charge, and things typically remain that way until someone leaves or someone is promoted. That is not the case on a High School football team. Every year new leaders must emerge. Every

year you have a new team. Old leaders graduate or move away and new leaders have to step up. For a team to be successful, you cannot have just two or three leaders – you must have an abundance of leaders. So, how do we get there? What can we do to make sure that our team this year has an abundance of good leaders?

The first thing we must do is establish a foundation for effective leadership and to do that we have to define what effective leadership looks like. There are thousands of books out there on leadership and I have read many of them. Leadership is a very technical skill and there are lots of good ways to develop into a great leader. However, I believe we tend to over complicate the idea of leadership. I thin think the foundation of effective leadership is best explained in one of my favorite stories.

Once upon a time two brothers who lived on adjoining farms fell into a conflict. It was the first serious rift in 40 years of farming side by side, sharing machinery, and trading labor.

One day the long collaboration began to fall apart. It began with a small misunderstanding and it grew into a major difference until it finally exploded into an exchange of bitter words followed by weeks of silence.

One morning there was a knock on the older brother's door. He opened it to find a man with a carpenter's toolbox. "I'm looking for a few day's work," he said.

Would you happen to have a few small jobs around your farm where I can help?"

"Yes," said the older brother. "I do have a job for you. Do you see that farm next door?" The carpenter replied, "yes." The older brother continued, "that farm belongs to my younger brother. He and I are no longer speaking. Do you see that creek running between our two properties?"

The carpenter looked at the small creek and replied, "yes." The older brother said, "there used to be a meadow between us. Last week my younger brother took his bulldozer and broke the levee to the river and now there is a creek between us. He did this to spite me. I want to do him one better. Do you see that pile of wood over by the barn?"

The carpenter once again replied, "yes." The older brother said, I would like for you to take that wood and build an 8 foot fence so I can see him and he can't see me."

The carpenter said, "I think I understand the situation. If you will show me to the nails and the post-hole digger, I will get to work."

The older brother had to go into town for supplies, so he got the carpenter set up and left for the day. The carpenter worked hard all day measuring, sawing, and nailing.

About sunset when the farmer returned, the carpenter had just finished his job. The farmer's eyes opened wide and his jaw dropped when he saw the final product.

The carpenter had not built a fence at all. Instead, he built the most beautiful bridge the farmer had ever seen. It stretched from one side of the creek to the other and it was a work of art. The hand rails were done perfectly. Every board was laid perfectly as well.

As the older brother looked at the bridge, he looked up to see his younger brother walking toward him with his hand outstretched.

"You are quite a guy to hire this fellow to build a bridge between us after all I have said and done," the younger brother said. The two brothers met in the middle of the bridge shaking hands and hugging.

As the older brother turned to find the carpenter, he saw him walking away in the distance. He called out to the carpenter saying, "wait, wait! I've got more jobs for you!"

The carpenter turned and waived a hand. He then called back and said, "I would love to stay, but I've got more bridges to build!"

In my opinion, effective leaders are bridge builders. They find ways to connect with those around them. When you have a team of bridge builders, you have incredible potential to accomplish great things. Every day you interact with people. Through the course of that interaction, you are either laying boards down on a bridge, or you are nailing boards up on a fence. Some people think to be an effective leader means you yell and scream and tell everyone what to do. That is not leading at all. That is fence building.

The more bridges we have from Upper Classmen to Lower Classmen, from Position to Position, from Players to Coaches, from Coaches to Players, and from Coaches to Coaches, the stronger we will be and the tougher we will be to beat. On the flip side though, if we spend more time building fences, then we will be easy to beat because we will fall apart the first time adversity shows up. The bottom line is you guys will ultimately decide whether we have more bridges on this team or more fences. I cannot be with you all of the time, listening to your conversations, or watching how you behave. It is in those moments that you have to decide what kind of a builder you are going to be. Just remember, the success of the team and your own individual success will be determined by whether or not we have more bridges than fences.

Personal Reflection

What do you think it takes to be a good leader?

_____

_____

_____

_____

Do you see yourself as a leader? Why or why not?

_____

_____

_____

_____

Who is the best leader you know personally?

_____

_____

_____

_____

What makes them a good leader?

_____

_____

_____

_____

What can you do in the next week to start becoming a better leader?

_____

_____

_____

_____

Be *the* Leader

YOU would follow!

Group Discussion

How many leaders do you need on your team? Why?

_____

_____

_____

_____

What type of leader do you respect the most?

_____

_____

_____

_____

Where does your school need more leadership?

_____

_____

_____

_____

How can you be a positive leader in your school?

_____

_____

_____

_____

What can you do as a team to improve your individual leadership skills?

_____

_____

_____

_____

Leadership is an

Action

Not a **Position**

As Coach discussed with his players in the story, the key to mastering the seven traits is to decide, define, and deliver. Take a moment now to do this when it comes to Leadership.

Leadership

Decide

I have within me the ability to be a great leader. I fully understand that to lead is to serve. Leadership is not defined by how good you are at a game, it is defined by how hard you work to help those around you. I will become a great leader by learning to be a bridge builder in the lives of those around me. I will defend, encourage, congratulate, and serve others in an intentional way each day. It is through those actions that I will be laying boards one by one on a bridge between my life and theirs. I refuse to be one who builds fences by being critical, judgmental, arrogant, and overly opinionated.

As a leader, I will recognize that everyone around me has value. When I notice someone doing something good or unselfish, I will make it a point to recognize what they have done and say Thank You. I fully realize that it is through these efforts that bridges are built, bonds are formed, and the foundation for me to become an effective leader has been laid.

When my foundation for being an effective leader is established, I will continue to work on the marks of good leadership. I will work each day to become proficient at my role, I will work to communicate well, I will display courage and a capacity to get things done, I will set an example with determination, foresight, and initiative, and I will work to be consistent in my self-discipline, responsibility, and respect for others.

Lastly, I will have high expectations for myself but I also realize that I cannot be perfect all of the time. The times when I make a mistake or I fail will be times where I learn something valuable. I will not allow my mistakes to rule my future. When I make a mistake, I will admit it, accept the consequences, and then move on. It is impossible to be a great leader or to accomplish great things without making some mistakes along the way. My mistakes will become opportunities to grow and through growing, I will become the leader I was meant to be.

I will build bridges. I will recognize the value in others. I will consistently work on the marks of a good a leader and I will turn mistakes into opportunities. I will become a great leader.

Define

I commit to avoiding the following things that would take away from my role as a leader:

_____

_____

_____

_____

_____

_____

_____

I commit to seeking out and pursuing the following things that will strengthen my resolve and motivate me to get better each day as a leader:

_____

_____

_____

_____

_____

_____

Deliver

In signing my name, I commit to reading this decision every morning and every night for 30 days, guarding my life from things that will weaken me as a leader, and filling my life with things that will help me continue to improve as a leader in life and on my team.

_____

Signature   Date

Session 12

Focus

The final trait of a winner is focus. Focus is the ability to control your mind, your attention, and your efforts towards accomplishing a specific task. Focus requires having a plan and then having the self-discipline, the motivation, and the persistence to stick to your plan. Let's see what Coach has to say about the final trait of a winner...

Always keep your target in mind. Then when life comes stampeding towards you, when problems seem overwhelming, you can go back to what you are shooting at and focus on that. As the problems present themselves, ask yourself, "What decision can I make in this situation that will take me closer to my goal?" It is that type of focus that will keep you heading in the right direction and allow you to face life's challenges.

Knowing what you are shooting at is the first part of focus. Once you have identified what you are shooting at, focus in on getting a little better each day. While keeping your big goal out in front of you, identify and focus in on the little things you can do each day to get you one step closer to the goal. Just like Major Sedgwick and his men, there had to be some urgency in order for them to learn something new and fight as hard as they did. When you set small daily goals that you can focus on, you create some urgency about meeting your goal before the day has ended. A logical question at this point would be, How can I guarantee that I am getting better each day? With that answer I am going wrap things up and thus wrap up The Classroom phase of our offseason.

The way to get better each day is to follow what we call "The Formula for Progress." The formula for progress is found in the book where the wisest of men look for answers – The Bible. It is found in Philippians 3:13-14. It goes like this:

"No dear brothers, I am still not all that I should be, but I am bringing all of my energies to bear on this one thing: forgetting the past and looking forward to what lies ahead, I strain to reach the end of the race and receive the prize for which God is calling me."

There are four points in those two verses that make up The Formula for Progress. They are clues on how to get better each day

The first point is found where it says, "No dear brothers, I am still not all that I should be…." Clue number one is Do Not Be Satisfied. The apostle Paul is the author of these verses and he was writing to a church in the city of Philippi. There was no question that the people of that church looked up to Paul and they aspired to be as accomplished as he was when it came to spreading the gospel. However, here he is telling them that he is not all that he should be. What does that say for the rest of us? We can all get better! If you are finally a senior, or finally a projected starter, or finally a returning letterman who has already won a State Championship, pay attention to the lesson Paul is teaching you. Do not be satisfied with where you are. There is always room to get better and we need you to get better each day if we are going to be the team we are capable of becoming.

The second point is found where he says, "….but I am bringing all of my energies to bear on this one thing…." Clue number two is also the Seventh Trait of a Winner – Focus on the Task at Hand. Whatever you are doing, focus on that one *thing. We live in a world that likes to use the phrase "multi-tasking." You might be able to do a lot of things at once, but that doesn't mean you are doing any of them well or to the best of your ability. If you choose to do something and it is important for your development, or it is something you need to get done in order to accomplish your goals, give it your full attention. Focus on the task at hand and then move to the next task.*

This is best exemplified in the course of a game. One game is made up of Two halves and those two halves are made up of four quarters. Those four quarters are made up of roughly 100 to 150 plays. If we play 15 games that will be 1500 to 2,250 plays by the end of the season. You cannot run play number 2,250 until you have run play number one and then play number two and so on. If we want to win our first game, we need to focus everything we have on winning play number one then we can focus everything we have on play number 2.

The team that is the best as a group at focusing on their job one play at a time is typically the one that wins the game. You have to play a season one play, one quarter, one half, one game at a time. That is true in life as well. You cannot accomplish your life goals all at one time. You have to work at it one day one project one lesson at a time. Focus on the task at hand and do that as well as you can possibly do it, then move on to the next task focusing on it.

The third point is found in the next phrase, "...forgetting the past..." Clue number three is to Forget the Past. You are going to make mistakes. We have already talked about that. Do not fear making a mistake. Understand that it is going to happen. The key is putting it behind you when that time comes. As you long as you are holding on to your past mistakes, you cannot move forward with what's next.

I have heard it said that the best quarterback is the one with short term memory loss. If he messes up and throws an interception, he forgets about it and moves on and it is imperative that he does so. Why? Because we may need him to lead a game winning drive later in the game. If he is still beating himself up over his past mistake, he will miss a great opportunity to be at his best when we need him the most.

This is also true in life. We have spent a lot of time over the last week talking about how to do things right. Inevitably, we have come across some things where you have told yourself "I am really failing in this area of my life." I want you to hear me loud and clear right now, Put it Behind you and Move On! If you have made mistakes, own up to them, learn from them, and move on! You cannot change the past, but you do have an opportunity to do better in the future. If you have been beating yourself up this week, it is time to move forward and let those things go. Make today the day that you start doing things differently. Make today the day that your life changes forever.

The final point is "…I strain to reach the end of the race and receive the prize for which God is calling me." The fourth clue is Total Effort. In everything that you do, give everything that you have. We talked about this when we talked about the trait of commitment. Those who lose consistently typically have a habit and giving half of what they've got just to save a little face if things don't work out. If you lose going half way or going all the way, you still lose. So, why not give your very best effort and put yourself on the line and then let the chips fall where they may.

You may not win every play or every game but at least you will have created a habit of doing your very best every time you take on a task. Work to make total effort a part of who *you are. It shouldn't matter if you are in math class, mowing the yard, or making a tackle – every time you do something, you give it your best effort.*

I sincerely believe that if you follow the formula for progress – if you refuse to be satisfied, if you focus on the task at hand, if you forget the past, and if you give your very best effort you will find that each and every day you will get a little better. When you add up all of those days of getting better, many years from now, you will look back and be amazed at how far you have come and all that you have managed to accomplish."

I believe in each one of you guys, I love each one of you, and I am proud to be your Coach. My prayer as we end The Classroom is the same as it was when we started. I pray that you find yourselves with a fertile heart and the seeds that have been sown this week will sprout inside you producing great things for you today, tomorrow, and for the rest of your lives.

Personal Reflection

Identify one goal that you are currently shooting for?

_____

_____

_____

_____

What do you need to focus on to accomplish this goal?

_____

_____

_____

_____

Do you have trouble forgetting the past and moving forward when you make a mistake?

_____

_____

_____

_____

Why is it important that you forgive yourself and move forward?

_____

_____

_____

_____

How can you "strain to reach the end of the race" when it comes to this season or this school year?

_____

_____

_____

_____

FOCUS ON BEING **Productive**

instead of **Busy**

Group Discussion

Where do you think you are currently becoming "satisfied" as Team?

_____

_____

_____

_____

Where do you think you need to get better as a Team?

_____

_____

_____

_____

What are you willing to do to help your team get better in this area?

_____

_____

_____

_____

What is one area where you need to be more focused?

_____

_____

_____

_____

What do you commit to do to help your team finish strong?

_____

_____

_____

_____

As Coach discussed with his players in the story, the key to mastering the seven traits is to decide, define, and deliver. Take a moment now to do this when it comes to Focus.

Focus

Decide

I am focused on the task set before me. Life might try to come at me in a way that is overwhelming, but I am up to the task. I know exactly what it is that I am shooting at and I will fight furiously to defend my position. Each morning when I wake up, I will remind myself of my goal, I will take aim, and I will start firing away at my target. If there are things in my life that are serving as distractions and they are seeking to take me further away from my target, I will remove those things from my life. My focus is clear. My hand is steady. Life can come at me as fast as it wants too. I am ready for the battle and I am focused on where I am going.

I understand a game can only be played one play at a time and the same is true in life. To win a game or to win in life, I need to focus on getting better each day. I will follow the formula for progress and make it my daily commitment.

I refuse to be satisfied with my current accomplishments. I am thankful for blessings of the past but I know there is more to do. I know there is more in me to give and I still have much to accomplish. Understanding that, I will focus on what is next and I will get better today.

I will focus all of my energies on the task at hand. If I am doing something, I will give it my full attention. If I am studying, I will focus everything I have on learning the material. If I am at practice, I will focus everything I have on mastering my position. If I am with friends, I will focus everything I have on being the best friend I can be. If I am in Church, I will focus everything I have on praising the Lord and thanking Him for the richness of his blessings.

I will forget the past and move on to a bigger and better future. I refuse to allow yesterdays failures to taint tomorrow's successes. Mistakes and failures are opportunities to learn. They are opportunities to grow and get better. I will make the most of those opportunities. I will learn my lessons and I will move on. The past will stay in the past and I will look ahead to a great future.

I will give everything that I have in all that I do. I understand that talent is given but success is earned. I will earn success because I will have worked hard for it. I will not hold back when I take on a task because it might not work out. Instead, I will put myself on the line, I will give my best effort and I will walk away - win or lose - with the satisfaction of knowing that I gave all I had to give.

Define

I commit to avoiding the following things that would serve as a distraction and weaken my focus:

_____

_____

_____

_____

_____

_____

_____

_____

I commit to seeking out and pursuing the following things that will strengthen my focus:

_____

_____

_____

_____

_____

_____

_____

_____

_____

Deliver

In signing my name, I commit to reading this decision every morning and every night for 30 days, guarding my life from things that will serve as a distraction and weaken my focus, and filling my life with things that will remind me of where I am going and what I am shooting for.

_____

Signature   Date

A Call To Coaches

I have been in and around the coaching profession for well over 40 years.

The most important time of my coaching career was when I realized that my work as a coach was a calling and a ministry from God.

I do not believe that it was ever the Lord's intention that the word of God be the exclusive property of professional clergy. All of us have our own little worlds and it's important to let God use who we are where we are.

We need to be men and women committed to Jesus Christ, penetrating society for Him. God uses laymen like you and me to reach into places where a minister cannot go, or if he could, he would not be as easily accepted.

What a tremendous responsibility we have, and it is more challenging today than it's ever been.

Coaches and athletics have always been at the forefront of social change. Playing sports has helped our country break down barriers of segregation and racism. It has brought the world together in times of war and has provided inspiration and optimism when our country needed it most.

Every coach is in a position that allows him to directly influence the attitudes of his athletes. Whether it is in team meetings, before and after practice sessions, or simply casual conversation, coaches have many opportunities to positively influence their players. It doesn't matter what sport you coach, your players look to you for leadership, guidance and instruction. Coaches through sports have a strong platform for delivering a message and positively impacting our students and schools.

It is my belief that there is no activity in our schools today that has any more carry-over value for adult life than competitive athletic programs. Athletes are the last stronghold of discipline we have left on our campuses today, and the leadership of our coaches has never been more important.

As coaches we must understand that the most important things that our athletic programs have to offer the educational process comes through using the platform of sports to teach winning attitudes, values and characteristics.

Sound athletic programs can provide valuable lessons for practical situations. The daily influential power of a positive coach can be life changing. Student athletes experience daily victories discovering within themselves the ability to overcome adversity, to develop leadership skills, to develop winning attitudes, to be hard workers, and to be a part of a team which requires sacrifice and service to others. These things are the direct results of quality coaching and the value of coaching kids on a daily basis, and are immeasurable qualities in helping them make strong choices and develop strong habits.

If a coach will use the platform that sports provides to teach not only the sport, but life skills and principles such as commitment, service, leadership, respect, responsibility and teamwork, we could change the downward slide of our country. This movement can come through a coaching profession that is united in its purpose.

You see, I believe that a coach has two tasks – one major and one minor – the major task is in the attitudes and character traits that we have an opportunity to teach. Our minor task is in teaching the skills and techniques of the game. All too often we get those two mixed up.

I believe that interscholastic sports are a very important part of the educational process. I also believe that we are in danger of losing our athletic programs as we know them today; and the only way for us to counter the negative scrutiny which athletics receive is by talking about the many good qualities of a sound athletic program.

We need to make it a point to speak up for athletics. We need to sell our programs and we need to point out to the people in our communities that our most important job is not in the skills that we teach, but the intangibles that we have an opportunity to teach like no other in education.

Intangibles such as:
- The development of strong character traits
- Teaching leadership skills
- Developing habits of commitment, dedication and sacrifice
- Teaching and developing selflessness, being a team player and care and concern for others
- Developing self-confidence
- Teaching the value of hard work
- Developing self-discipline

- Developing the skill of handling adversity
- Teaching the importance of a proper mental attitude

I think sometimes as coaches we pass over these intangibles as being "corny" – BUT THEY'RE NOT! These are the most important things that our athletic programs have to offer the educational process.

Outside of parenting there is not a stronger platform to teach these life lessons than coaching. As coaches we need to find the time and the ways to teach and develop these intangibles. We need to take them away from some of their "strength and conditioning" and put them in "the classroom" to teach and develop these attitude and character traits.

I was nervous when we first started the classroom and unsure of how it would be received, or if it would even work. However, the years of success at Judson proved that it did work, and it worked on multiple levels. Our kids were not only successful on the field, we watched them go on and become successful in life and lead families of their own. The opportunity to see the impact of "the classroom" in the kids we coached was a far greater reward than any game we ever won. I promise you, if you will do a good job with "the classroom" in your own program, your athletes will find ways to work on their strength and conditioning on their own time.

Coaches, it is my prayer that you will see coaching as more of a mission than a profession. You have an opportunity to make a difference in the lives of young people every single day. The influential power of the coaching profession is significant and the responsibility that goes along with it is even more significant. I commend you on answering the call to coach, now I challenge you to get out there and coach everyday in a way that proves to all who see that you are – Coaching to Change Lives.

D.W. Rutledge

About the Author

Clint Rutledge is the son of legendary High School Football Coach D.W. Rutledge. Growing up around the Judson program, Clint eventually went on to become an All City player in both baseball and football at Judson High School. During his time there he helped lead the Judson Rockets to back to back State Championships as a quarterback on their 1992 and 1993 Football teams.

Clint then went on to Baylor University where he graduated with a double major in History and English. After graduating, he went back to Judson to serve as their quarterbacks Coach where he won his Third State Championship medal in 2002.

In 2005, he left the coaching profession and entered the business world as a Real Estate Agent. Clint is now one of the top Realtors for Keller Williams Realty in the greater San Antonio area. He currently serves in multiple leadership roles in New Braunfels including the New Braunfels Christian Academy School Board, Deacon at Oakwood Baptist Church, Monthly Speaker on Leadership Development for Department Heads in the City of New Braunfels, Steering Committee member for Youth Leadership New Braunfels, Monthly Speaker for Youth Leadership New Braunfels, Monthly Speaker for the Adult Leadership New Braunfels, Director of the All Pro Dad's Program at New Braunfels Christian

Academy, Co-Author of <u>The Family Plan</u>, and the Founder and Director of The Fourth Quarter Leadership Institute an innovative new leadership training for High School and College athletes.

In 2014, Clint was awarded the Chair of Board award for significant contributions in the area of Youth Leadership Development in the City of New Braunfels. Clint has been married to his wife Jamie for 16 years and he has three kids, daughter Raylee age 13, son Ryder age 11, and daughter Reese age 3.

To book Clint for a speaking event, you can contact him by email or through his website at <u>www.ClintRutledge.com</u>.

Notes

Session One

1. Luke 8:1-15

2. Susan Hawkins, "The Cold Within" by James Patrick Kinney: Poem. Purpose, Progress. *http://www.allthingsif.org/archives/1405*.

Session Two

1. Chuck Swindoll, https://www.goodreads.com/author/quotes/5139.Charles_R_Swindoll

The Story of the Stonecutter, http://edbok.com/2012/05/the-parable-of-the-stonecutter/

Session Three

1. Bruce Lowitt, St. Petersburg Times: "Wrong Way Reigels takes off into History", http://www.sptimes.com/News/92699/Sports/_Wrong_Way_Riegels_t.shtml

Session Four

1. Zig Ziglar; *See You At The Top*; (Pelican Pub Co Inc; Revised & Enlarged edition June 1982)

2. Start Where You Stand; https://allpoetry.com/Start-where-you-stand

Session Five

1. Andy Andrews; *The Noticer Returns*; (Thomas Nelson Publishers October 8, 2013)

2. Paul Aurandt, Jr.; Paul Harvey's The Rest of the Story;

http://www.geocities.ws/ryanpbrunner/paulharveyros.html

Session Six

1. Vicki Huffman; *Plus Living*; (Harold Shaw Publishers,1989)

Session Seven

1. Chuck Swindoll; *The Quest for Character*; (Zondervan Publishing House) p. 17-18

Session Eight

1. Larry Burton; "It don't cost nothin to be nice";

http://bleacherreport.com/articles/61880-it-dont-cost-nothin-to-be-nice

Session Nine

1. *Rashika Jain Inspirations; Story of the Bridge Builder;*

http://rishikajain.com/tag/inspirational-story/page/3/

2. Motivate Us.com; "Puppies for Sale";

http://www.motivateus.com/stories/puppies.htm

3. The Bridge Builder;

https://www.poetryfoundation.org/poems-and-poets/poems/detail/52702

Session Ten

1. Coaches Outreach; Study of
2. Philippians 3:13-14; The Formula for Progress

Notes

Notes

Notes

Notes

Notes

Notes

58982608R10096

Made in the USA
Columbia, SC
31 May 2019